I0105752

birdsong
a musical field guide

alexander liebermann
foreword by austin kleon

First Edition Published 2022

All transcriptions and text © 2022 Alexander Liebermann, unless otherwise noted
Foreword © 2022 Austin Kleon
Illustrations © 2022 Anna Schiller
Cover Design by Benjamin Jackson © 2022 Just a Theory Press
All Rights Reserved.

No part of this book may be reproduced by any means without written permission
from the publisher, except brief portions quoted for purposes of review.

Published by
Just a Theory Press
Ann Arbor, MI 48105
www.justatheorypress.com

ISBN 979-8-9854386-0-4

Designed and produced by Just a Theory Press
Printed in the U.S.A. by McNaughton & Gunn

10 9 8 7 6 5 4 3 2 1

CONTENTS

FOREWORD

"It's probable that in the artistic hierarchy birds are the greatest musicians existing on our planet. Birds are the first and the greatest performers."

—Olivier Messiaen

During the early days of the pandemic, people turned to hobbies to help them get through their days. Some people started bird-watching. Some people picked up musical instruments. Alexander Liebermann did a combination of both: he used his musical ear to transcribe birdsong into sheet music.

This book freezes birdsong on the page so you can examine it, think about it, and then listen for it when you're out in the world. It's worth pointing out that "bird-watching" is a somewhat inaccurate term. A veteran birder will tell you that if you want to see birds, the first thing you should do is listen for them. Bird-watching is often a matter of bird-listening. Once you learn to find birds with your ears, you can find them with your eyes.

What's funny to me about these transcriptions is that most of them are near impossible to play. (I read the book at my piano, stopping to try out a line here and there.) Like a John Cage score, the transcriptions function, essentially, as a form of conceptual art. You don't really have to be able to read music to get what you need out of them. If you look at the pages as you would a piece of art, you will see the music of birds.

Birdsong is one of my favorite kinds of books, a mashup of two subjects with multiple entry points for readers. Birders will learn something about music, musicians will learn something about birds, and readers who know nothing of either will be inspired to open up their ears and listen.

—Austin Kleon

Author's Note

When the COVID-19 pandemic started, I left New York City to travel to Germany, where I am originally from. While I spent my days at home in Berlin, completely isolated, it was difficult for me to stay inspired and to compose music. One day, however, I stumbled upon a YouTube video that showed different animals and their calls. I found solace in these creatures' vocalizations, particularly in birdsong, and I started transcribing them to sheet music.

Almost immediately, working with birdsong proved to be more than just a distraction from quarantine life: it became a way for me to stay inspired and productive. The infinitely rich gestures and melodic elements in birdsong fueled my creativity, increased my productivity, and ended my writer's block.

I started uploading my transcriptions to social media, where—to my surprise—musicians from around the world began to perform them. I thought, if transcribing birdsong is so helpful to me, maybe it can help others, too. Thus came the idea of this book: a volume designed to convey to the reader the same joy and sense of wonder that I feel and, in doing so, serve as a similar source of inspiration for other curious and creative people, regardless of their background or expertise.

This volume features ten birdsong transcriptions, each accompanied by a brief description of the species, an illustration by artist Anna Schiller, and a QR code. These QR codes will direct the reader to different YouTube videos showing the original birdsong and its musical notation. In some cases, the videos will include a vocal or instrumental interpretation of the transcription.

Finally, I want to remind the reader that I relied entirely on my ears to transcribe the following birdsong. Basic music software sometimes helped me to slow down recordings and to split sound files, but at no point in the transcription process did I use specialized scientific instruments. Consequently, this book should not be seen as a scientific book but rather as a musician's personal and humble attempt to put nature's symphony to sheet music.

—Alexander Liebermann

ACKNOWLEDGEMENTS

This book would not have been possible without the love and encouragement of my parents. From the youngest age, they taught me to appreciate music, treasure education, and stay curious and open-minded. They have supported me on my musical path ever since I played my first note, for which I will never be able to thank them enough.

My gratitude also goes to all the incredible teachers with whom I was fortunate enough to study. Everything I know about music they taught me, and this book would not have been feasible without their teaching and guidance. A special shout-out goes to my ear training teachers Manfred Hüneke, Kyle Blaha, and Wayne Oquin, who showed me that one can improve in this subject and, above all, have fun.

Lastly, I want to acknowledge the invaluable help I received in writing this book. I am grateful to Joshua DeVries for his great ideas and his hard work in publishing this book, Stephanie Sodero for her excellent insights and comments, and my friends Matthew Graybil, Johannes Neumann, Matthew Ricketts, and Rory Varrato, who read the first full draft of the book and made valuable suggestions for improvement.

NOTE ON THE TRANSCRIPTIONS

1. All the transcriptions are written in treble clef. In some transcriptions, the clefs are labeled with **8**^{va} and **15**^{ma} signs (𝄞 and 𝄞) for legibility.

2. The x-shaped noteheads (♩) indicate that the sound produced is percussive and contains a lot of noise.

3. The microtonal notation used in the transcriptions is limited to the following accidentals: ♭ ↓♭ ♮ ♯ ↑♯. These accidentals do not indicate an exact cent alteration in pitch, rather a direction in which the note deviates from the well-tempered system.

4. The rehearsal marks indicate either a clear, lengthy time separation between two parts of the same song or a song from another bird of the same species.

Birdsong

A Musical Field Guide

Musician Wren "Uirapuru"

(Cyphorhinus arada)

Musician Wren "Uirapuru" — Cyphorhinus arada

The musician wren is a small brown songbird native to the Amazon rainforest of Brazil. It is famous for its beautiful song and for the stories and myths that surround it. This legendary bird has even found its way into concert halls thanks to the many composers who have been inspired by it (including Heitor Villa-Lobos, Olivier Messiaen, and François Bayle).

The vocalizations of the uirapuru are very haunting. Every single bird has a unique call sung with eventual variety (repeating a song-type several times before switching to another), yet all demonstrate a common preference for perfect consonances. Intervals such as perfect octaves, perfect fifths, and perfect fourths tend to be more frequently used than dissonances and imperfect consonances. That is one of the reasons why a vast majority of us will perceive its song as "tonal."

I was fascinated to find a parallel between rhythmic units of the birdsong and Brazilian music. The syncopated pattern ♪♪♪, typically associated with Samba, is very recognizable in this transcription. I am sure this is a coincidence, but I like to remember that cultures from all over the world, such as the Tuvans and the ancient Chinese, have attributed the origins of music to birds and other animals. Similarities between the sounds of nature and music might be more common than we think!

Birdsong – A Musical Field Guide

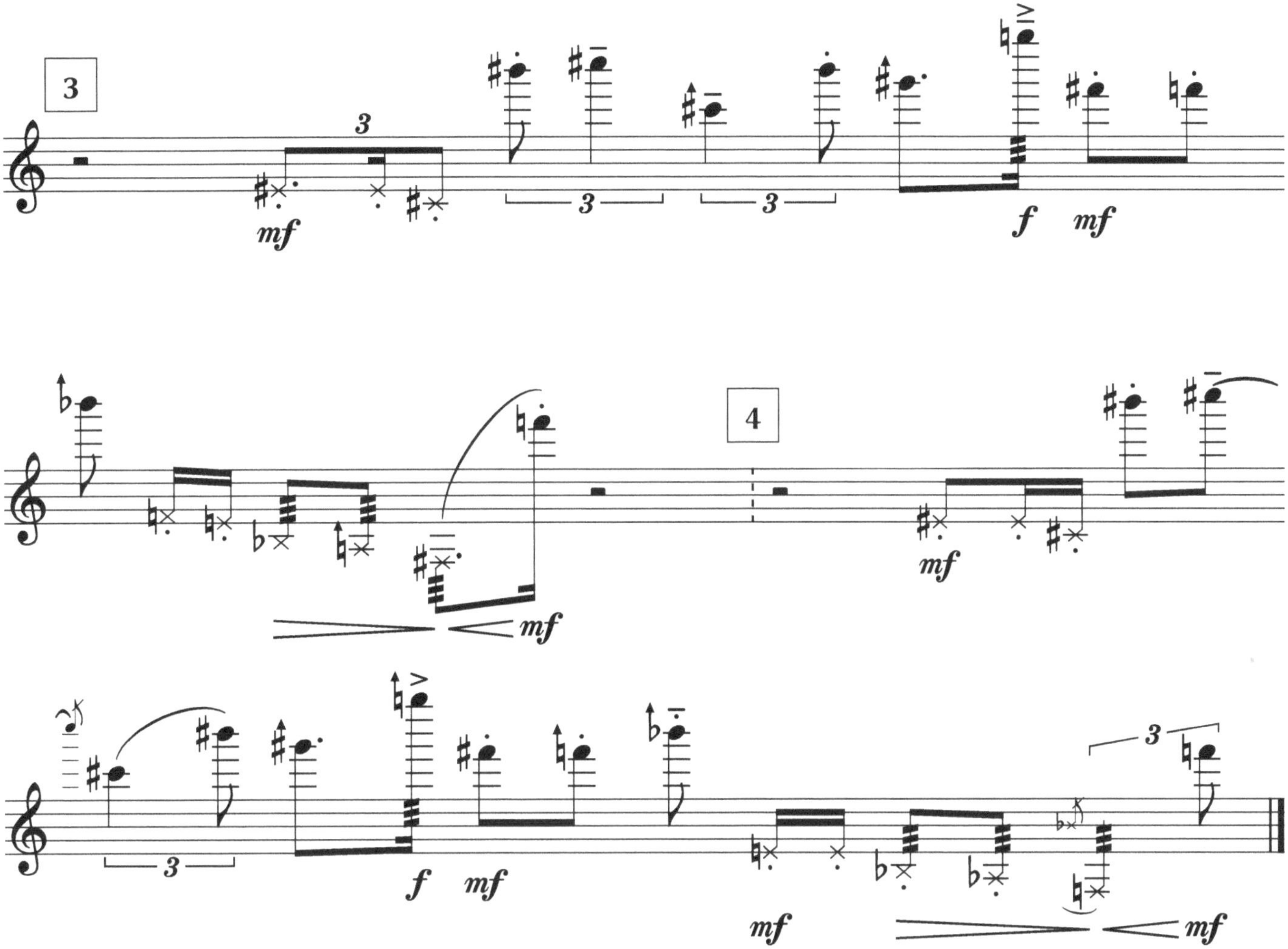
3
mf
f
mf
4
mf
mf
f
mf
mf
mf

Nightingales

(Genus Luscinia)

Common Nightingale

(Luscinia megarhynchos)

Common Nightingale — Luscinia megarhynchos

The common nightingale travels between 1,550 and 2,800 miles every year to breed in Europe, Northwest Africa, and Southwest Asia. To secure and establish a territory in time, male nightingales always return from their overwintering grounds south of the Sahara—anywhere from West Africa to Uganda—before the females.

The song of the male nightingale has been described as one of the most striking of all birds in the world. It varies by season and circumstances but is at its richest, loudest, and most magnificent in late spring when the bird sings to proclaim territory and to attract a mate.

There are two distinct categories of vocalizations: whistle songs and non-whistle songs. The frequency of whistles can go as high as 8 kHz, roughly corresponding to the note B8, which is an octave above the highest note on the piano! If my ears have not deceived me, then the A♯ in rehearsal number ⑤ is close to the highest possible whistle note, which means that you will not be able to play it on the piano unless you transpose it down an octave.

The nightingale has inspired many composers, and countless pieces refer to the bird and its song. Franz Schubert's *An die Nachtigall* and Igor Stravinsky's *Song of the Nightingale* are among my favorites.

Birdsong – A Musical Field Guide

Common Nighingale

Thrush Nightingale

(Luscinia luscinia)

Thrush nightingale — Luscinia luscinia

In Northeastern Europe and Asia lives a bird very similar to the common nightingale: the thrush nightingale. Due to their similarity in appearance and song, these species are challenging to differentiate. However, the following subtleties can help you distinguish them:

1. The song of the thrush nightingale is usually more resonant than the one of the common nightingale, but it is less melodic and contains fewer harsh sounds.

2. Although both species can be found in the woods near water, the thrush nightingale clearly prefers lowlands and generally avoids arid areas.

3. Unlike its relative, the thrush nightingale has faint gray breast spots, like those of the song thrush (hence the name), and duller upper parts.

When comparing the transcriptions of the two birds, I find it interesting that the upward intervallic leaps at the end of phrases are significantly larger with the thrush nightingale than with the common nightingale. Compare the ending of rehearsal number ⊡ in both transcriptions to see this difference.

Birdsong – A Musical Field Guide

Thrush Nightingale

EMPEROR PENGUIN

(Aptenodytes forsteri)

Emperor Penguin — *Aptenodytes forsteri*

The emperor penguin is the largest of all penguin species. It spends its entire life in the coldest region on Earth and is the only animal known to breed during the harsh Antarctic winter.

After laying a single egg, each female passes it to her mate, who covers it with a fold of skin to keep it warm. The females then head out to the sea. For the next two months, all the male penguins huddle together through the winter gales, eating nothing throughout the entire incubation period. As a result, during this time, they lose up to 50% of their body weight! The males set off to feed only when the females return to feed the newly hatched chicks. Once they have regained their strength, the males return and resume parental duties.

During courtship, the male and female penguins trumpet loudly to each other and learn each other's distinctive call. This technique helps them identify their mates amidst breeding colonies of up to 40,000 penguins.

Adult emperor penguins typically use both sides of their syrinx (birds' vocal organ) simultaneously, producing vocalizations using two voices. In contrast, our single voice box (larynx) only allows us to perform one tone at a time. In the videos that serve as the basis for these transcriptions, the calls of adult penguins mainly consist of two-voice vocalizations using intervals such as seconds and thirds. In contrast, the chicks' peeps consist of single voices outlining numerous intervals, including thirds, fourths, fifths, and sixths.

Birdsong – A Musical Field Guide

like an old car failing to start

BUTCHERBIRDS

(Genus Cracticus)

GREY BUTCHERBIRD
(*CRACTICUS TORQUATUS*)

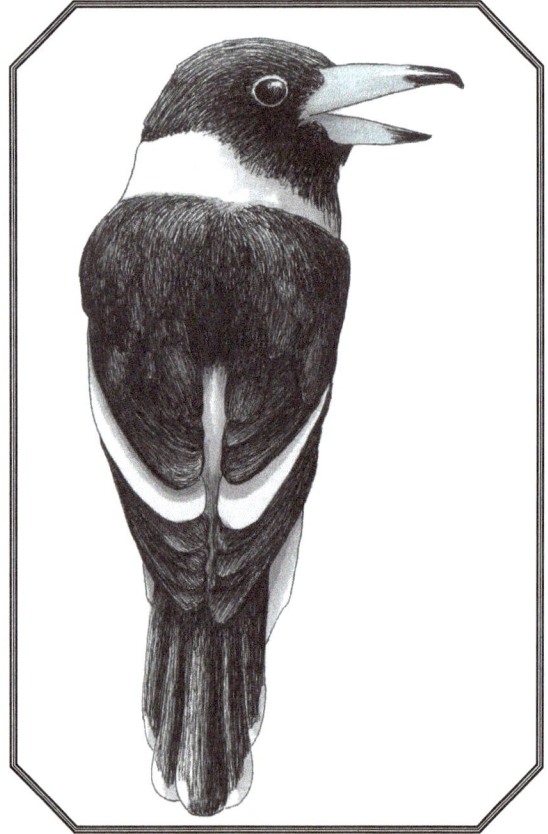

PIED BUTCHERBIRD
(*CRACTICUS NIGROGULARIS*)

BUTCHERBIRDS — GENUS CRACTICUS

These Australian birds are bold, aggressive, and highly vocal. They owe their common name "butcherbird" to their habit of wedging prey between wire fences or in tree forks, which allows them to tear apart larger animals than would otherwise be possible. The generic name *Cracticus* comes from the ancient Greek word *Kraktikos* (meaning "noisy") and thus refers to their strident calls.

Of the six species in the genus, two are featured in this book: the grey butcherbird (*Cracticus torquatus*) and the pied butcherbird (*Cracticus nigrogularis*).

The following songs are very rhythmic and contain well-defined intervals with clean intonation. It is not surprising that the French composer Olivier Messiaen—famous for having worked with birdsong—took an interest in their vocalizations. Especially the call of the pied butcherbird fascinated Messiaen, so he incorporated it in *Éclairs sur l'au-delà*, his last work.

Grey Butcherbird

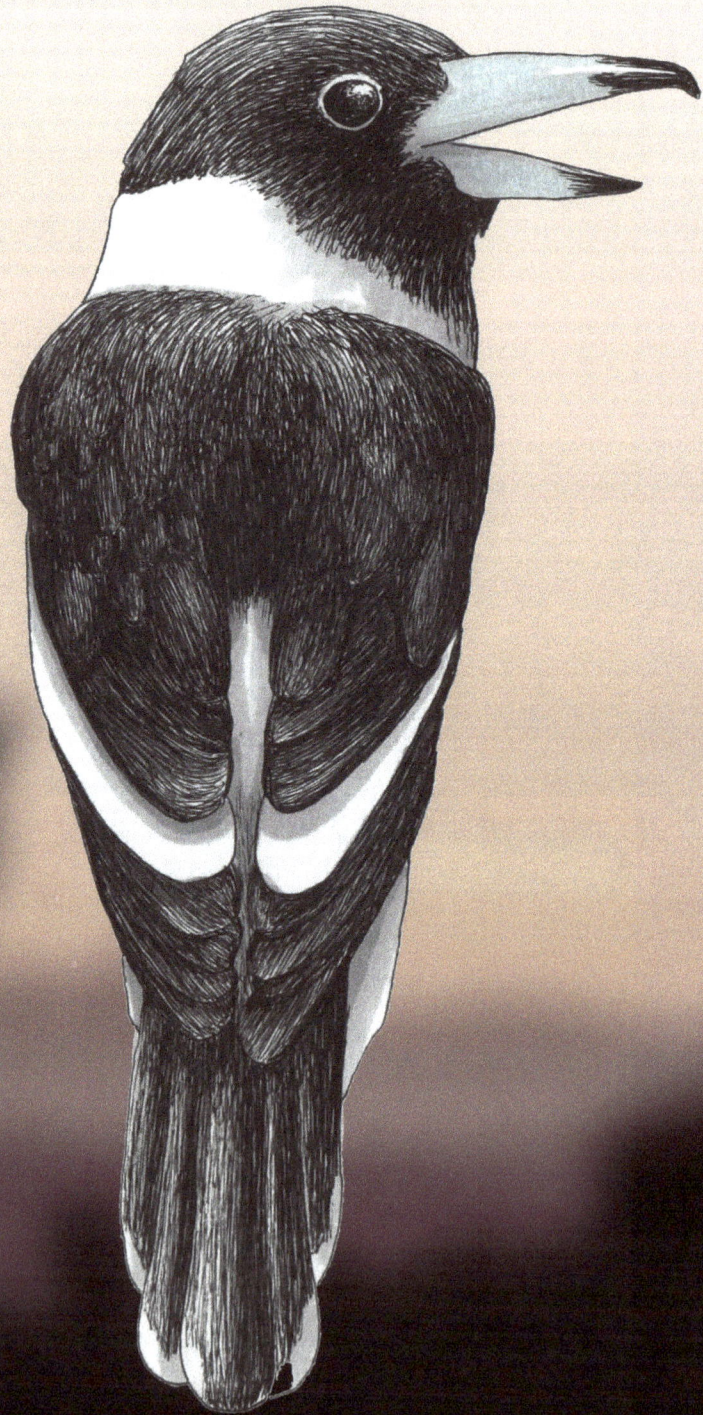

Great Reed Warbler

(Acrocephalus arundinaceus)

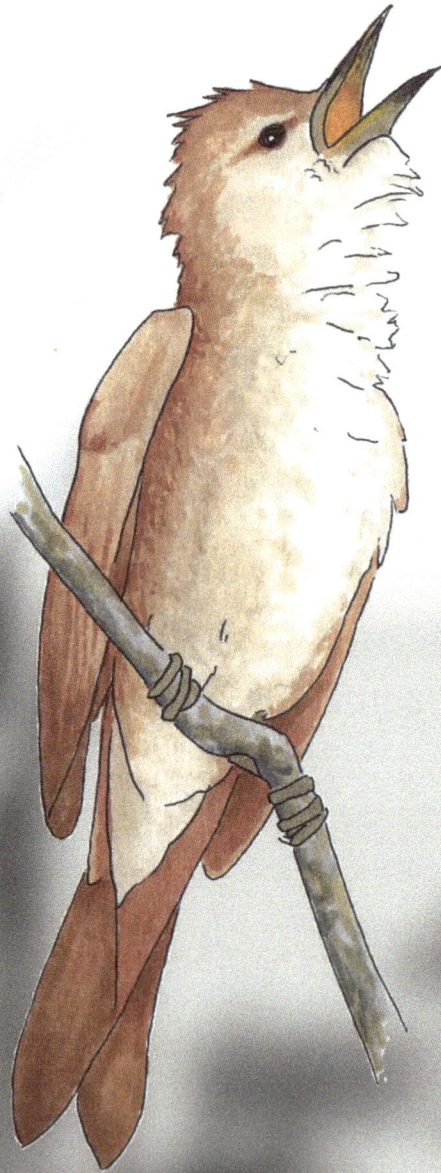

GREAT REED WARBLER — *ACROCEPHALUS ARUNDINACEUS*

The great reed warbler is a medium-sized bird with a vast breeding range extending from South-West Europe to Asia's Pacific coast. It winters in Sub-Saharan Africa, anywhere from Sierra Leone to southern Ethiopia and South Africa.

With long, narrow wings ensuring an energy-efficient flight, and feet made of three short toes in front and one long toe in the back, the great reed warbler is perfectly built for a life spent perching among reedbeds and undertaking long migrations.

The male communicates via two primary song types: (1) short songs of about one second with low-amplitude syllables and (2) long songs of about four seconds with a vast array of high-amplitude elements added to the short song structure. Males primarily use long vocalizations to attract females, while short ones tend to be used for territorial encounters with rival males.

like the sound of
a camera shutter

bells up!

Birdsong – A Musical Field Guide

almost like a jackhammer

COMMON CUCKOO

(Cuculus canorus)

Common Cuckoo — Cuculus canorus

The common cuckoo is a particularly widespread summer bird in Europe and Asia that migrates to Africa in winter. The bird is an obligate brood parasite, which means that the females lay their eggs in the nests of various other bird species.

In 2002, a study found that 64% of great reed warbler nests in central Hungary were parasitized with cuckoo eggs. However, for the cuckoo, laying an egg in a warbler nest is no risk-free endeavor. Cuckoos caught in the process can fall victim to merciless torture, as evidenced by the following testimony:

> *The cuckoo was pushed into the water; the great reed warbler stood on the top of the cuckoo's head and attacked it continuously with his beak until the bird became unconscious and drowned in the water.*[1]

The male's infamous song is typically given from an open perch during the breeding season. It consists of vocalizations of 1–1.5 seconds in length, occurring in groups of 10 to 20 with a few seconds of rest between groups. The song is generally first heard in April, when it consists of a descending minor third. The interval gets wider as the season progresses, reaching up to a perfect fourth in May. In June, the cuckoo stops singing its infamous tune and makes other calls, including some that incorporate ascending intervals. Can you guess in which month the cuckoo sang this call?

---

1 From Thomas Oliver Mérő & Antun Žuljević, "*Great Reed Warbler Acrocephalus arundinaceus*," in "*Acrocephalus*," 130.

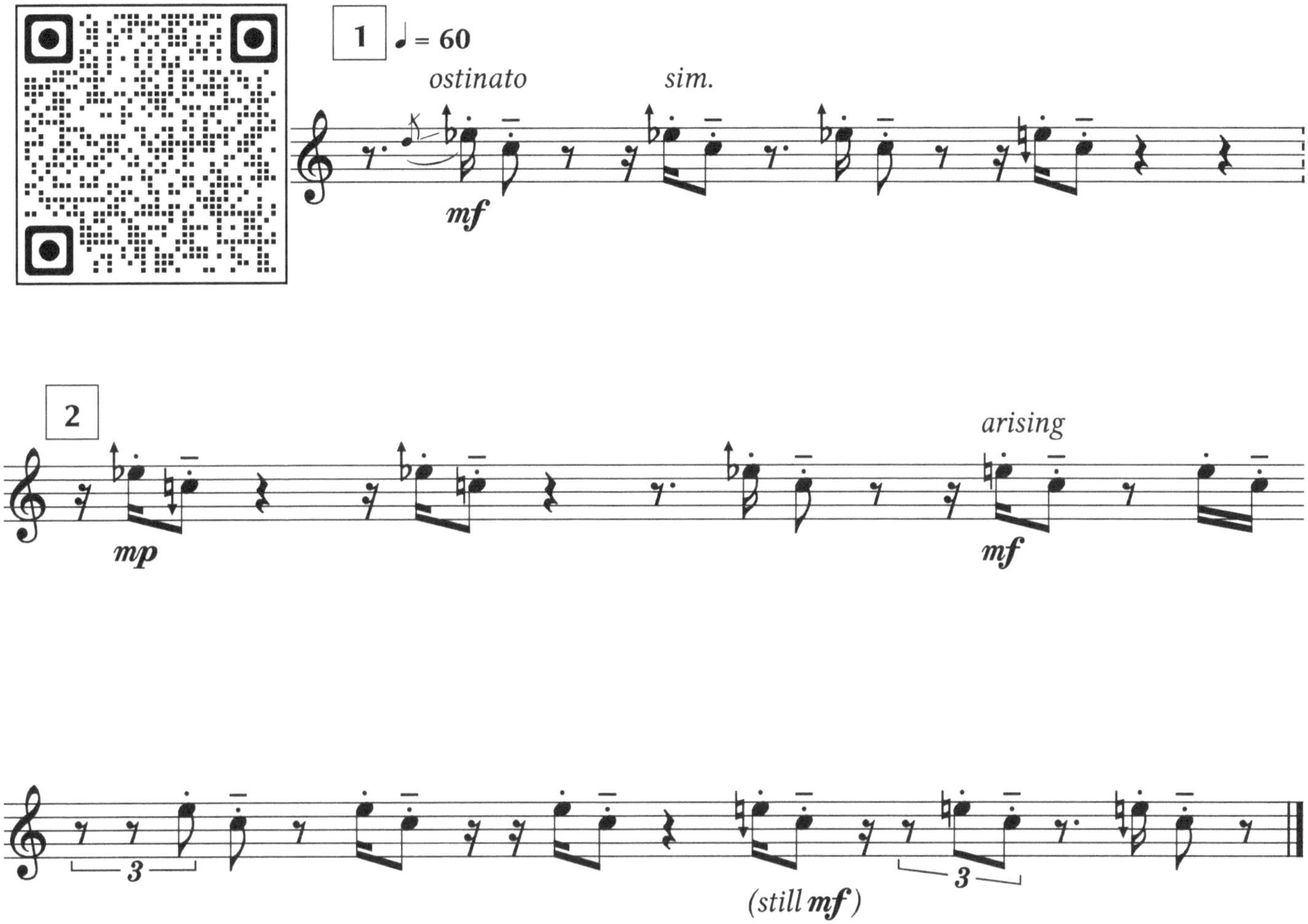
1
♩ = 60
ostinato
sim.
mf
2
mp
arising
mf
3
(still mf)

Japanese Bush Warbler
"Uguisu"

(Cettia diphone)

Japanese Bush Warbler "Uguisu" — Cettia diphone

The Japanese bush warbler, also known as Uguisu, is an Asian songbird native to Japan and the northern Philippines. Depending on the season, it can also be found in China, Korea, and Taiwan. It was introduced to Oahu in the 1930s, from whence it spread to the main Hawaiian Islands.

The Japanese bush warbler is a secretive bird. It prefers to spend its time hidden in the foliage rather than on exposed branches. The bird is consequently more often heard than seen, and the best time of year to spot it is in spring before the trees bloom.

In early spring, the Japanese bush warbler's distinctive breeding song (rehearsal mark 1) echoes throughout much of Japan, where it is imitated onomatopoeically with the sound "hooo-hokekyo." The beauty and richness of its song led to the English name "Japanese nightingale," which can be misleading because—unlike the common nightingale and the thrush nightingale—the Japanese bush warbler is *not* a nightingale and does not sing at night.

Japanese Bush Warbler "Uguisu"

Savi's Warbler

(Locustella luscinioides)

Savi's Warbler — Locustella luscinioides

The Savi's warbler is a small bird of the order Passeriformes, a large order containing more than half of all bird species. It is typically found in reed beds near bushes and is a migratory bird; it breeds in Europe and the Western Palearctic and winters in Northern and Sub-Saharan Africa.

The common name acknowledges the Italian ornithologist Paolo Savi, who wrote the first complete description of the bird in 1824. The genus name *Locustella* is from the Latin *Locusta*, meaning "grasshopper," and describes the quality of its call. *Luscinioides* combines the Latin word *Luscinia* ("nightingale") and the ancient Greek affix '-*oides*' ("resembling").

The song of Savi's warbler is insect-like and high-pitched, consisting of a monotonous flux of regular clicks similar to the buzzing of a sewing machine. It resembles the song of the grasshopper warbler, but is much faster and lower-pitched, and does not have the same ringing quality (due to less prominent high frequencies).

The following call keeps surprising me—a seemingly fragile bird merely 5.5 inches long manages to hold a loud pitch for 41 seconds without ever changing the dynamic. Do not try this at home!

About the Author

Alexander Liebermann is music theory and ear training faculty at Juilliard's preparatory division Music Advancement Program. A composer and passionate nature lover, he began transcribing animal sounds to sheet music in the early days of the COVID-19 pandemic. His original and accurate transcriptions are viral on social media and have been featured in the world-renowned magazine National Geographic.

www.alexanderliebermann.com

Anna Baptist

www.ingramcontent.com/pod-product-compliance
Lightning Source LLC
Chambersburg PA
CBHW042341030426
42335CB00030B/3421